Zero Carb Recipes to Delight Your Taste Buds and Boost Your Health

Unlock a Whole New World of Delicious Meals with this Zero Carb Diet Cookbook

BY

Remi Morris

+++++++++++++++++++

Copyright Notes

Table of Contents

Introduction

Don't let a low-carb diet make you feel like your taste buds are doomed to a life of monotony and boredom! Break free from the mundane and introduce some delicious excitement with this revolutionary zero-carb cookbook. This book is sure to whet your appetite and bring joy back to mealtime.

You will learn the secrets of creating delicious and wholesome meals. In this zero carb cookbook, there are no processed or refined carbs. Learn over thirty delicious dishes that are made with healthy, all-natural ingredients. Enjoy an invigorating home-cooked meal every night with these simple yet hearty dishes. Say goodbye to store-bought convenience food and start cooking with real, nutrient-rich ingredients, it's time to experience the truth about zero-carb cooking!

Some of the tastiest dishes actually contain zero carbs, which may come as a surprise if you're on a weight-loss diet. It's true: even if you eat like a king, you can still drop pounds. This cookbook has 30 tempting dishes for you to try.

IIIIIIIIIIIIIIIIIIIIIIIIIIIIIIIIIIIIIIIIIIIIIIIIIIIIIIIIIIIIIIIIIIIIIIIIIIIIIIIIIIII

1. Beef Tips in Crockpot

Makes: 8 servings

Cooking Time: 8 hours and 10 minutes

Ingredient List: -

- Stew meat (2 lbs. Lean)
- Lipton onion soup mix (2 envelopes)
- Mushroom soup (2 cans, 10.5 oz., 98% fat-free)
- Red wine (1 cup; beef broth can be used as a substitute)
- Sliced mushrooms (2 cans; 8 oz., drained)

||||||||||||||||||||||||||||||||||||||||||||||||||||||||||||||||||||||||||||||||||||||||

How to Cook: -

a. In a crock pot, combine all of the
b. Cook them on a low setting for a period of 6-8 hours.

2. Low Carb Cabbage Rolls

Makes: 12 cabbage rolls

Cooking Time: 5 hours and 10

Ingredient List:

- Cabbage leaves (12, Napa)
- Beef (1 lb., ground)
- Parmesan (1 cup)
- Garlic (2 cloves, minced)
- Onion powder (1 teaspoon)
- Parsley (1 handful)
- Pepper (1/2 teaspoons)
- Marinara sauce (1 cup, no sugar added)

||||||||||||||||||||||||||||||||||||||||||||||||||||||||||||||||||||||||||||

How to Cook:

a. Set a saucepan over a high heat setting with about a cup of water and allow it to come to a boil. Once it is boiling, add in your cabbage and cook it until it is slightly tender (about 3 minutes) then quickly leave the vegetable to cool.

b. Pour half of your marinara into your slow cooker.

c. Now let's make some cabbage rolls! Begin by combining all of your ingredients except for the cabbage and marinara sauce in a medium bowl and stir to combine them together.

d. Lay your cabbage leaves on a flat surface and spoon your filling evenly into the leaves. Roll your cabbage leaves to create a roll then place them seam-side down in your slow cooker.

e. Top them with the remaining marinara sauce and set the cooker to cook on a medium heat setting for a period of 5 hours. Enjoy!

3. Apple Cinnamon Slow Cooker Oatmeal

Makes: 4 servings

Cooking Time: 6 hours and 10 minutes

Ingredient List:

- Apples (2, peeled, sliced)
- Cinnamon (1 teaspoon)
- Stevia (1/3 cup)
- Rolled oats (2 cups, old–fashioned)
- Water (4 cups)
- Salt (a pinch)

||||||||||||||||||||||||||||||||||||||||||||||||||||||||||||||||||||||||||||||

How to Cook:

a. Add your apple slices into your slow cooker, and top them with cinnamon, and stevia, then stir to combine the ingredients.
b. Evenly add in your rolled oats then top this with salt and water. Do not stir!
c. Allow the ingredients to cook on a low setting for a period of 9 hours.
d. Stir, serve and enjoy the apple cinnamon slow-cooked oats!

4. Keto Slow Cooker Breakfast Casserole

Makes: 4 servings

Cooking Time: 6 hours and 15 minutes

Ingredient List: -

- Eggs (6 large)
- Bacon (3 slices)
- Shallot (3 tablespoons, chopped)
- Red Bell Pepper (½ cup, chopped)
- Mushroom (1 cup, chopped, white)
- Kale (8 large leaves, finely shredded)
- Butter (1 tablespoon)
- Parmesan cheese (1 cup shredded)
- Salt and pepper, to taste

‖‖

How to Cook:

a. Set a skillet with your bacon in it, over high heat and allow it to cook until it becomes crispy. Once it is crispy add your shallots, red pepper, and mushrooms then sauté these ingredients until they become fork tender.

b. Next, add in your kale, remove your pot from the heat, and allow it to just

c. Whisk together the salt, pepper, and eggs until they are fully incorporated.

d. Set your slow cooker to a high setting and in your butter. Use the melted butter to grease the inside of your slow cooker.

e. Add your vegetables, then top them with your cheese and eggs.

f. Stir, cover, and leave the ingredients to cook for a period of 6 hours on the lowest setting. Enjoy!

5. Paleo Slow Cooker Breakfast Casserole

Makes: 6 servings

Cooking Time: 6 hours and 10 minutes

Ingredient List:

- Coconut oil (2 tablespoons)
- Leek (1 ⅓ cups, sliced)
- Garlic (2 teaspoons, mince)
- Kale (1 cup, chopped)
- Egg (8 large)
- Butternut squash (⅔ cups, peeled, cored, grated)
- Beef sausage (1 ½ cups)

||||||||||||||||||||||||||||||||||||||||||||||||||||||||||||||||||||||||||||

How to Cook:

a. Set a skillet with coconut oil over medium heat and let it

b. Once it has fully melted, add in your garlic, kale, and leeks then sauté them until they are fork tender.

c. Combine all of your ingredients, including your cooked veggies, and place them into your slow cooker basket then add all of the eggs, butternut squash, beef sausage, and sautéed vegetables.

d. Allow this to cook for a period of 6 hours on a low setting. Serve, and enjoy.

6. Keto Slow-Cooker Beef & Broccoli

Makes: 4 servings

Cooking Time: 6 hours and 15 minutes

Ingredient List:

- Flank steak (2 lbs., sliced in 2" chunks)
- Coconut aminos (2/3 cup)
- Beef broth (1 cup)
- Stevia (3 tablespoons)
- Ginger (1 teaspoon, grated)
- Garlic (3 cloves, minced)
- Red Pepper Flakes (1/2 teaspoons)
- Salt (1/2 teaspoons)
- Broccoli (1 head, chopped in florets)
- Bell pepper (1, red, cut into 1" pieces)
- Sesame seeds (1 teaspoon, garnish)

||||||||||||||||||||||||||||||||||||||||||||||||||||||||||||||||||||||||||||||||

How to Cook:

a. Set your slow cooker to pre-heat on a low setting.

b. Add all of your ingredients, except for the vegetables, and sesame seeds, and leave them to cook for about 5 hours.

c. Add your vegetables, stir and resume cooking for another hour on low.

d. Top this with sesame seeds, serve, and enjoy!

7. Slow Cooker Veggie Frittata

Makes: 4 servings

Cooking Time: 4 hours 10 minutes

Ingredient List:

- Eggs (6)
- Paleo Vegan Cheese (½ cup)
- Nutritional Yeast (1 tablespoon)
- Mushrooms (4 oz., sliced)
- Spinach (¼ cup, fresh, chopped)
- Italian seasoning (2 teaspoons)
- Cherry tomatoes (1/4 cup, sliced)
- Green onions (2, sliced)
- Ghee (1 teaspoon)

How to Cook:

a. Use cooking spray to lightly grease your slow cooker basket.

b. Heat a medium skillet over medium heat on the stove and add ghee to melt it. Once it has fully melted, add in your vegetables then sauté them until they are soft.

c. Pour your vegetables into your slow cooker.

d. Combine your cheese, eggs, and seasonings in a medium bowl and whisk to combine everything together.

e. Add your egg mixture into your slow cooker and set it to cook on the lowest setting for a period of 4 hours.

8. Slow Cooker Maple Apple Butter

Makes: 1 quart

Cooking Time: 8 hours and 10 minutes

Ingredient List:

- Apples (8 cups, chopped)
- Lemon (1, juiced)
- Cinnamon powder (1 tablespoon)
- Allspice (1 teaspoon, powder)
- Clove (1 teaspoon, powder)
- Ginger (1 teaspoon, powder)
- Nutmeg (1/4 teaspoon, ground)
- Water (1 1/2 cups)
- Maple Syrup (1/2 cup)
- Salt (1 pinch)

‖‖‖

How to Cook:

a. Add all of your ingredients to your slow cooker, stir, and allow it to for a period of 8 hours on a low setting (or until your mixture has reduced by half).

b. Allow the mixture to cool, then transfer it to your blender and process it until it is smooth.

c. Store this in an airtight container and refrigerate it until you are ready to use.

9. Crockpot Mexican Breakfast Casserole

Makes: 10 servings

Overall: 5 hours and 15 minutes

Ingredient List:

- Pork Sausage Roll (12 oz.)
- Garlic Powder (1/2 teaspoon)
- Coriander (1/2 teaspoons)
- Cumin (1 teaspoon)
- Chili powder (1/2 teaspoon)
- Salt (1/4 teaspoons)
- Pepper (1/4 teaspoons)
- Salsa (1 cup)
- Eggs (10)
- Almond Milk (1 cup, unsweetened)
- Pepper Jack cheese (1 cup)

||||||||||||||||||||||||||||||||||||||||||||||||||||||||||||||||||||||||||||||||

How to Cook:

a. Cook your meat, and sausage until they have fully cooked, over medium heat in a large skillet.

b. Pour in your seasonings and salsa then set this aside.

c. Add your milk, and eggs together in a separate bowl and whisk to combine.

d. Add your cheese, meat, and sausage mixture to the eggs, and stir.

e. Pour your eggs into a greased slow cooker and allow them to cook on a low setting for a period of 5 hours. Enjoy.

10. Paleo Slow Cooker N'Oatmeal

Makes: 1 serving

Cooking Time: 8 hours and 10 minutes

Ingredient List:

- Walnuts (1/2 cup, raw, soaked)
- Almonds (1/2 cup, raw, soaked)
- Butternut squash (1 medium, peeled and cubed)
- Apples (2 apples, peeled and cubed)
- Cinnamon (1 teaspoon)
- Nutmeg (1/2 teaspoons)
- Coconut Sugar (1 tablespoon)
- Coconut milk (1 cup)

Toppings:

- Maple syrup (1 teaspoon, 100% maple syrup)

|||||||||||||||||||||||||||||||||||||||||||||||||||||||||||||||||||||||||||||||

How to Cook:

a. Add your soaked nuts to a food processor and pulse them into a flour-like

b. Add all of your ingredients to your slow cooker and allow them to cook for a period of 8 hours on a low setting.

c. Use a potato masher to mash the N'Oatmeal into your preferred consistency.

d. Top it with maple syrup and serve.

11. Easy Russian Slaw

Makes: 6 Serving

Cooking Time: 22 Minutes

Ingredient List:

- White cabbage (¼ medium head)
- Red cabbage (¼ small head)
- Celeriac (½)
- ½ fennel bulb (½)

Russian dressing:

- Mayonnaise (⅓ cup)
- Coconut milk (2 tablespoons)
- Sriracha chili sauce (1 tablespoon)
- Cucumber (1 medium, pickled)
- Grated horseradish (1 teaspoon)
- Lemon juice (2 tablespoons, fresh)
- Parsley (2 tablespoons Freshly chopped)
- Chives (2 tablespoons, freshly chopped)
- Salt to taste
- Freshly ground black pepper

How to Cook:

a. Wash the cabbage and fennel and slice them thinly.

b. Peel the celeriac, grate it, and put it in a medium-sized mixing bowl along with the cabbage and fennel.

c. In another container, prepare the Russian dressing. Grate the horseradish and pickled cucumber very finely. Add the mayo, coconut milk, lemon juice, Sriracha sauce, parsley, and chives. Season to desired taste with salt and pepper.

d. Add the dressing to the cabbage mix and combine thoroughly. Enjoy!

12. Slow Cooker Bacon, Egg & Hash Brown Casserole

Makes: 8 servings

Cooking Time: 3 hours and 15 mins

Ingredient List:

- Frozen hash browns (20 oz. Bag, shredded)
- Bacon (8 slices, cooked; coarsely chopped)
- Cheddar cheese (8 oz., shredded)
- Green onions (6, sliced thin)
- Eggs (12)
- Milk (½ cup)
- Salt (½ teaspoons)
- Pepper (¼ teaspoons)
- Cooking oil (enough to grease the slow cooker lightly)

||||||||||||||||||||||||||||||||||||||||||||||||||||||||||||||||||||||||||||||

How to Cook: -

a. Use cooking oil to grease your slow cooker lightly.
b. In the bottom of the slow cooker, lay half of the hash browns and use half of the following ingredients: cheese and bacon, as well as a third of the green onions to top the hash browns. Set the remaining portion of ingredients aside for garnishing.
c. After topping them, repeat this process with another bed of hash brown, cheese, green onion, and bacon.
d. In a large bowl, whisk together the eggs, milk, pepper, and salt. Pour this mixture slowly over the hash browns in the crock pot.
e. Cook them on a high setting for a period of two to three hours until the eggs have hardened, or on a low setting for a period of four to five hours.
f. Dredge the hash browns with the leftover bacon and onions and serve them instantly. They can also be served with some hot sauce on the side.

13. Grilled Vegetable Salad with Olive Oil and Feta

Makes: 4 Servings

Cooking Time: 25 Minutes

Ingredients

- Eggplant (1 medium, sliced ¼" thick)
- Zucchini (1 medium, sliced ¼" thick)
- Bell pepper (1, red, cut into 1/2-inch strips)
- Extra virgin olive oil (3 tablespoons)
- Garlic (2 cloves, minced)
- Sea salt (¾ teaspoons)
- Cracked black pepper (½ teaspoons)
- Dried oregano (½ teaspoons)
- Crumbled feta (½ cup)

||||||||||||||||||||||||||||||||||||||||||||||||||||||||||||||||||||||||||||

How to Cook:

a. Preheat the grill to a medium temperature. Place the sliced vegetables on a preheated grill and allow them to cook for a period of 4 mins on each side. Cook them until they are tender or the edges become slightly charred.

b. Remove the veggies from the grill and put them to the side to cool. Chop them into small pieces (½ inch) and place these pieces into a bowl.

c. Add garlic, olive oil, oregano, salt, and pepper to the vegetables, and stir to coat them. Cover them with feta cheese and toss this slightly.

d. Tip: The eggplant can be salted half an hour before cooking it to reduce any bitter taste and aid in cooking

14. Slow Cooker Lower Carb Cabbage Roll Stew

A tasty home-style recipe for slow cooker lower carb cabbage stew.

Makes: 10 servings

Cooking Time: 6 hours and 15 mins

Ingredient List: -

- Ground beef (1 lb., extra lean)
- Onion (1 medium, chopped)
- Stewed tomatoes (1 can; 14.5 oz.)
- Tomato sauce (1 can; 14 oz; low sodium)
- Garlic (1 tablespoon, minced)
- Worcestershire sauce (1 tablespoon)
- 1 cup low sodium chicken broth (1 cup; low sodium)
- Black pepper (1 teaspoon)
- Hot chili flakes (½ teaspoons)
- Cabbage (½ head, chopped)

||||||||||||||||||||||||||||||||||||||||||||||||||||||||||||||||||||||||||||||

How to Cook: -

a. Brown the beef and onions in a medium size pot. Place all of the ingredients in a slow cooker (except for the cabbage and browned beef and onion) and combine them together well.

b. Add the browned beef and onions, then add the

c. Cook these ingredients for a period of 5-6 hours on a low setting.

15. Twice Baked Spaghetti Squash

Makes: 4 Servings

Cooking Time: 1 Hour 10 Minutes

Ingredient List:

- spaghetti squash (2 small to medium)
- olive oil (2 tablespoons)
- onion (1 small, chopped)
- marinara sauce (1 pint)
- sausage (½ lb., Italian)
- baby spinach (1 bag)
- Mozzarella (1 cup)
- Parmesan (½ cup)
- salt and pepper

IIIIIIIIIIIIIIIIIIIIIIIIIIIIIIIIIIIIIIIIIIIIIIIIIIIIIIIIIIIIIIIIIIIIIIIIIIIIIIIIIIIIIIIIII

How to Cook:

a. Heat the oven to a temperature of 400°F. Slice the spaghetti squash lengthwise in halves (from the stem to the tail). Remove all of the seeds and stringed flesh.

b. On a flat baking tray, place the squash and dribble it with 1 tablespoon of oil. Sprinkle all salt and a dash of pepper all over it and leave it to bake in the oven for a period of 40 mins. (smaller squashes will take less time).

c. In the meantime, in a large skillet, sauté the chopped onions in olive oil, over a medium flame. Sauté them for a period of five minutes or until the onion becomes translucent.

d. Add the sausage and cook it until it becomes brown; then add the marinara sauce. When the sauce becomes bubbly, stir in the spinach by handfuls, until all are wilted (this should take a period of one or two minutes). If the squash is not ready at this point, turn off the heat, remove the skillet, and put it aside until the squash has finished cooking.

e. As soon as the squash comes out of the oven, gently, pull the flesh from the peel with a fork. The flesh will be separated into threads.

f. If the squash is proving difficult to scrape, return it to the oven for a further 10 minutes. Pull your fork in the same direction by raking it through the strands to produce the longest "noodles."

g. Toss the noodles (made from squash), into the sauce mix, then return the noodles to the peels.

h. Top each half of the squash with some Return them to the oven to bake for a period of 15 mins., just until the cheese is bubbly.

16. Slow Cooker Balsamic Chicken

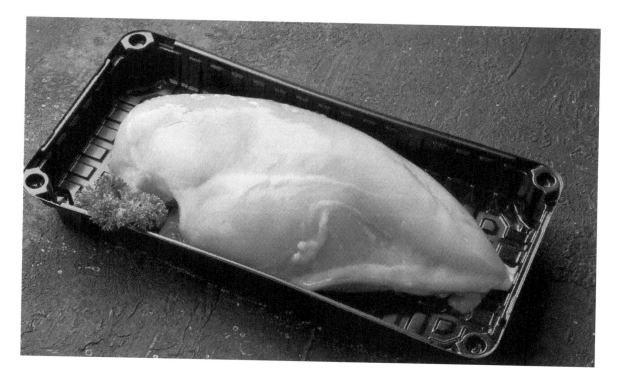

Makes: 10 servings

Cooking Time: 4 hours and 15 minutes

Ingredient List:

- Chicken breasts (3 lbs. Boneless and skinless)
- Diced tomatoes (2 cans, 14.5 oz.)
- Medium onion (1 medium, thinly sliced)
- Garlic (4 cloves)
- Balsamic vinegar (½ cup; for gluten-free use white balsamic vinegar)
- Olive oil (1 tablespoon)
- Dried oregano (1 teaspoon,)
- Dried basil (1 teaspoon)
- Dried rosemary (1 teaspoon)
- Thyme (½ teaspoons)
- Ground black pepper for seasoning according to personal preference
- Salt for seasoning according to personal preference

||||||||||||||||||||||||||||||||||||||||||||||||||||||||||||||||||||||||||||

How to Cook: -

a. Pour the olive oil onto the bottom of the slow cooker.,

b. Place the chicken breasts into the slow cooker, and sprinkle salt and pepper on each piece of breast.

c. Place the sliced onion on top of the chicken; then add in all dried herbs and cloves of garlic. Pour in the balsamic vinegar and place the tomatoes on top.

d. Cook the chicken for a period of 4 hours on a high setting. Serve the cooked balsamic chicken over pasta.

17. Mediterranean "Pasta"

Makes: 4 Servings

Total Time: 20 Minutes

Ingredient List:

- Zucchini (2 large, spiral sliced)
- Spinach (1 cup, packed)
- Olive oil (2 tablespoons)
- Butter (2 tablespoons)
- Garlic (5 cloves, minced)
- Sea salt and black pepper, to taste
- Tomatoes (¼ cup, sun-dried)
- Capers (2 tablespoons)
- Italian flat leaf parsley (2 tablespoons, Italian flat leaf, chopped)
- Kalamata olives (10, halved)
- Parmesan cheese (¼ cup, shredded)
- Feta cheese (¼ cup, crumbled)

||||||||||||||||||||||||||||||||||||||||||||||||||||||||||||||||||||||||||||||||

How to Cook:

a. Place the spinach, zucchini, butter, garlic, olive oil, black pepper, and sea salt, in a large saucepan.

b. Over a medium flame, sauté everything until the zucchini becomes tender and the spinach quails. Drain off the excess liquid.

c. Add the capers, parsley, sun-dried tomatoes, and Kalamata olives. Combine these ingredients and sauté them for a period of 3 minutes.

d. Remove the saucepan from the Sprinkle Parmesan and feta cheese over the pasta and toss it before serving the Mediterranean pasta.

18. Sausage and Sweet Pepper Hash

Makes: 8 servings

Cooking Time: 6 hours

Ingredient List: -

- Smoked chicken sausage (12 oz. Pk.)
- Olive oil (1 teaspoon)
- Sweet onion (1 ½ cups, sliced)
- Nonstick cooking spray
- Red-skinned potatoes (1 ½ lb., sliced into 1/2-inch pcs)
- Fresh thyme (2 teaspoons, snipped)
- Ground black pepper (½ teaspoons)
- Chicken broth (¼ cup, reduced sodium)
- Chopped green, red, and/or yellow sweet peppers (1 ½ cups)
- Shredded swiss cheese (½ cup, optional)
- Parsley (2 teaspoons, snipped)

||||||||||||||||||||||||||||||||||||||||||||||||||||||||||||||||||||||||||

How to Cook: -

a.   In a suitable nonstick skillet, cook the sausage over medium flame until it turns brown in color. Remove the cooked sausage and set it aside.

b.   Using the same skillet, warm up some oil over a medium-low heat setting.

c.   Add the sliced onion and sauté it for roughly a period of 5 minutes or until the onion slices are tender. Make sure to stir them occasionally.

d.   Spray the bottom of a 4-quart slow cooker with some cooking spray or line it with a slow cooker disposable liner.

e.   In the slow cooker, add the sausage, potatoes, onion, black pepper, and thyme, and combine all of the ingredients. Add the broth to the mixture in the cooker.

f.   Set the cooker to a low heat setting, cover it with a lid and leave the ingredients to cook for a period of 5-6 hours on a low heat setting or you can cook them on a high heat setting for a period of 2 ½ to 3 hrs.

g.   Toss in the colored peppers. If cheese is to be used, sprinkle some over the sweet peppers.

h.   If you are using the low-heat setting, turn the cooker to the high-heat setting at this point. Cover the cooker with a lid and leave the ingredients to cook for an additional period of 15 mins.

i.   Sprinkle the sausage and sweet pepper hash with parsley before serving. A slotted spoon should be used for serving.

19. Grain-free Mac and Cheese

Makes: 6 Servings

Cooking Time: 1 Hour and 5 Minutes

Ingredient List:

- Creme fraiche (½ cup)
- Heavy cream (½
- Yellow mustard (2 tablespoons)
- Teaspoon sea salt (½ teaspoons)
- Black pepper (½ teaspoons)
- Jicama (1 lb., cut into ¼" x ¼" x 1" pieces)
- Onion (½ cup, minced)
- Sharp cheddar cheese (3 cups, shredded)

||||||||||||||||||||||||||||||||||||||||||||||||||||||||||||||||||||||||||||||

How to Cook:

a. Place the heavy cream, sea salt, creme fraiche, black pepper, and yellow mustard in a medium-sized mixing bowl. Stir until the ingredients are well-combined.

b. Add in the jicama and minced onion and coat.

c. Lastly, add the shredded cheese and combine until all of the ingredients are properly blended.

d. Scrape this mixture into a small ovenproof greased baking dish.

e. Bake the dish in the oven for a period of 50 minutes and bake at a temperature of 350°F.

f. Once this time has passed, remove the grain-free mac and cheese from the oven and serve it right away while it is still hot.

20. Crockpot Thai Beef Stew

Makes: 6-8 servings

Cooking Time: 5-8 hours

Ingredient List:

- Coconut oil (2 tablespoons, divided)
- Beef stew (3 lbs., trim fat)
- Yellow onion (1 medium., thinly sliced)
- Garlic (2 cloves, minced)
- Fresh ginger (2 teaspoons, scraped and minced)
- Full-fat coconut milk (1 can, 13 1/2 oz, full fat.)
- Tomato paste (⅓ cup)
- Thai red curry paste (½ cup, Thai red)
- Fish sauce (2 tablespoons)
- Fresh lime juice (2 teaspoons)
- Sea salt (2 teaspoons)
- Peeled and julienned jicama (1 cup)
- Julienned carrots (2 cups)
- Broccoli florets (2 cups)
- Fresh cilantro, for garnish

||||||||||||||||||||||||||||||||||||||||||||||||||||||||||||||||||||

How to Cook:

a. In a large skillet placed over a medium-high flame, heat up 1 tablespoon of the coconut oil. Brown the meat in batches (as everything cannot hold in the skillet all at once), on all sides.

b. Transfer the batches of browned meat to the slow cooker using a slotted spoon. Continue to brown the beef.

c. To ensure even browning of the meat, between the browning of the batches, wipe out the skillet to get rid of any excess fluid gathered at the bottom.

d. Wipe out the skillet; pour in the remaining coconut oil and sauté the garlic, ginger, and onion for a period of five minutes.

e. Add in the coconut milk and continue stirring it until the browned bits on the bottom of the pan are released.

f. Combine the curry paste, tomato paste, salt, fish sauce, and lime juice. Pour this mixture over the beef in a slow

g. Cook the beef for a period of five hours on a high setting or for a period of 8 hours on a low setting.

h. During the final 30 mins. of cooking, add the carrots, broccoli, and jicama, or in the final hour if you are using a low setting. Use cilantro to garnish and serve the crockpot Thai beef stew.

21. Paleo Slow Cooker Chicken & Kale Soup

Makes: 4 servings

Cooking Time: 6 hours and 5 minutes

Ingredient List:

- Chicken thigh/breast (2 lbs. Skinless, boneless)
- Chicken bone broth (3 ½ cups, homemade)
- White onion (1 medium, chopped)
- Garlic (4 cloves, smashed)
- Shredded carrots (1 ½ cups, shredded)
- Kale (4 cups, chopped)
- Parsley (1 ½ teaspoons)
- 1 1/2 teaspoons Parsley
- Salt and pepper for seasoning according to personal preference

||||||||||||||||||||||||||||||||||||||||||||||||||||||||||||||||||||||||

How to Cook:

a. Clean and wash the whole chicken thighs/breasts and place them in the slow cooker.

b. Lay the onions over the chicken, and add the garlic and chicken bone broth. The secret to the yummy flavor of this delicious soup is in the homemade bone broth. (If the homemade bone broth is not available at the time of cooking the soup, use bone-in chicken instead. You will get all the health benefits plus a richer taste. Remove the bones when the soup is done).

c. Let the chicken, onions, garlic, and broth cook on a low setting for about 4 to 6 hours.

d. The chicken will start coming apart. Use a fork to assist in separating the chicken into chunks.

e. Add the carrots, parsley, kale, and pepper & salt to taste. Cook for a further period of 1 hour.

f. Once this time has passed, remove the Paleo chicken from the slow cooker and serve it. Enjoy!

22. Orange Cinnamon Beef Stew

Makes: 4 servings

Cooking Time: 2½ hours and 20 mins

Ingredient List:

- Beef stew (2 lbs grass-fed. Cut in 1" pcs and pat dry)
- Salt (1 teaspoon) + pepper (1 teaspoon)
- Coconut oil (2-3 tablespoons)
- Medium onion (1 medium, diced)
- Carrot (1, diced)
- Celery (1 stalk, diced)
- Garlic (2 cloves, minced)
- Orange (½ cup plus zest)
- Balsamic vinegar (¼ cup)
- Water (4 cups)
- Ground cinnamon (2 teaspoons)
- Bay leaves (3)
- Rosemary (1 tablespoon, finely chopped)
- Fresh thyme (1 tablespoon, finely chopped)
- Fresh sage (1 tablespoon, finely chopped)
- Small rutabagas (4 small, spiralized)

||||||||||||||||||||||||||||||||||||||||||||||||||||||||||||||||||

How to Cook:

a. Heat the oven to a temperature of 350°F.

b. In a Dutch oven, heat coconut oil over a medium-high Add a layer of the meat pieces ensuring that there is enough space in between each piece. Dribble the pieces with some pepper and salt and fry them until all sides turn golden brown in color. Transfer the cooked meat pieces to a plate and set them aside. Continue cooking the meat in batches until all of the pieces are done, add more oil if necessary so that the bottom of the pot does not burn or stick.

c. After the pieces of meat have been browned and removed from the Dutch oven; place the onions, celery, carrot, and garlic in a pot and sauté them until the vegetables are fragrant, or for roughly a period of 1. min.

d. Add the orange juice and mix this well. Now, add the browned meat, zest, water, balsamic vinegar, salt, cinnamon, bay leaves, and pepper.

e. Bake this in the oven until the meat is extremely tender, almost falling apart, for roughly a period of 2 - 2 ½ hours.

f. Mix in thyme, rosemary, and sage and cook the meat for a further period of 10-15 minutes.

g. In the meantime, place the rutabaga into a steaming basket; add a pinch of salt and steam it over a pot of boiling water for about 5 minutes, until it is firm.

h. Serve the orange cinnamon beef stew immediately (for a tasty boost of healthy fat, add a dribble of extra-virgin olive.)

23. Paleo Beef & Pumpkin Stew

Makes: 4 servings

Cooking Time: 6 hours and 5 mins

Ingredient List:

- Steak (¾ lb., stewing)
- Pumpkin (½ lb.)
- Coconut oil (6 tablespoons)
- Sage (1 teaspoon)
- Mixed herbs (1 teaspoon)
- Rosemary (2 teaspoons)
- Thyme (2 tablespoons)
- Salt & pepper for seasoning according to personal preference

‖‖

How to Cook:

a. Set the slow cooker on a high setting. Remove the excess fat from your stewing steak and place the steak in the slow cooker. Add 3 tablespoons of coconut oil; rub in a dash of pepper and salt. Put the cooker to cook for a period of 60 mins at a high temperature.

b. Transfer the steak from the slow cooker to a bowl. Add the seasoning and the remaining portion of coconut oil and combine thoroughly. Return the meat to the slow cooker along with the pumpkin and cook it for another period of 3 hours on a low setting.

c. Garnish the Paleo beef and pumpkin stew with fresh herbs and serve.

24. Easy Avocado & Egg Salad

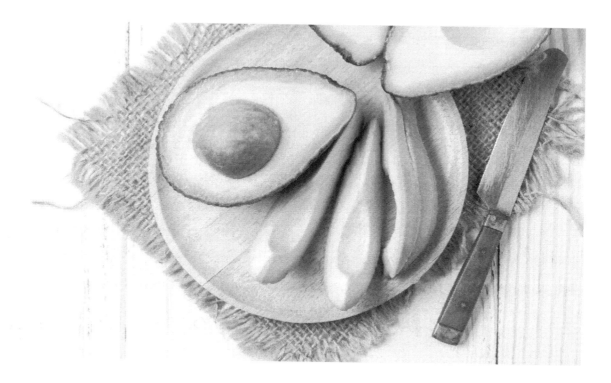

Makes: 2 Servings

Cooking Time: 15 Minutes

Ingredient List:

- Eggs, (4 large, organic)
- Avocado (1 large)
- Mixed lettuce (4 cups, arugula, lamb lettuce, etc.)
- Mayonnaise (¼ cup)
- Garlic (2 cloves, crushed)
- Dijon mustard (2 teaspoons)
- Salt and pepper for seasoning according to personal preference
- Fresh herbs, chives, extra virgin olive oil (optional; for garnishing)

||||||||||||||||||||||||||||||||||||||||||||||||||||||||||||||||||||||||||

How to Cook:

a. Let us first cook the eggs by filling a small saucepan three-quarters of the way with water. Add a little salt to protect the eggs from cracking. Add the eggs and allow them to boil.

b. Turn off the heat as soon as the pot starts boiling. Cover it with a lid and let the eggs stand for a period of 10 minutes.

c. When the eggs have finished cooking, place them in some cold water. Peel off the shell when the eggs have fully

d. To make the dressing, mix together Dijon mustard, mayonnaise, and crushed garlic and season it with a pinch of salt and pepper.

e. Wash the greens, drain and pat them dry using a paper towel. Put the greens in a salad bowl and blend them with the dressing. Cut the avocado into halves, remove the seeds, peel, slice and arrange the pieces on top of the greens.

f. Lay the egg quarters on top and if necessary season with more salt and pepper. Enjoy the easy avocado and egg salad!

25. Chili Pulled Pork Tacos

Makes: 10 servings

Cooking Time: 8 hours

Ingredient List:

- Pork butt/shoulder (4 ½ lbs.)
- Chili powder (2 tablespoons)
- Kosher salt (1 tablespoon)
- Ground cumin (1 ½ teaspoons)
- Ground oregano (½ teaspoons)
- Crushed red pepper flakes (¼ teaspoons)
- A pinch of ground cloves
- Stock or broth (½ cup)
- Bay leaf (1)

||||||||||||||||||||||||||||||||||||||||||||||||||||||||||||||||||||||||||||||||

How to Cook:

a. Combine the oregano, chili powder, cumin, salt, cloves, and red pepper flakes in a mixing bowl.

b. Clean and wash the pork and put it on a clean platter. Rub the spice mix thoroughly on all sides of the pork using your hands. Make sure the pork is fully coated with the spice mixture.

c. Leave the pork to marinate overnight in the refrigerator or for at least a period of two hours minimum if time is against you.

d. Place the marinated pork in a slow cooker with the stock/broth and bay leaf. Set the cooker to cook on a low setting for a period of 8 hours.

e. When the time has passed, separate the pork from the liquid and place the pork on a cutting board. Use 2 forks to shred the

26. Keto Crock Pot Chicken Soup

Makes: 4 servings

Cooking Time: 6 hours and 10 minutes

Ingredient List:

- Onion (1 medium, chopped)
- Celery (3 stalks, diced)
- Carrots (3 medium, diced)
- Apple cider vinegar (1 teaspoon)
- Fresh Herbs (1 tablespoon fresh)
- Chicken breasts (2 organic, bone-in, skin-on)
- Chicken thighs (2 organic, bone-in, skin-on)
- Sea salt (1 teaspoon)
- Fresh ground pepper (½ teaspoons)
- Filtered water (3-4 cups)

||||||||||||||||||||||||||||||||||||||||||||||||||||||||||||||||||||||||

How to Cook:

a. Arrange all of the ingredients in the same order listed in a suitable size crockpot; place the chicken bone side down on top of the vegetables.

b. Pour enough water to fully cover the vegetables and let the water come halfway up to the chicken. Cook the chicken and the vegetables on a low setting for a period of 6-8 hrs.

c. Take out the chicken from the pot and let it cool slightly. De-bone the chicken and take off the skin. Use a fork to tear the meat apart and add it to the soup in the crockpot. Adjust the seasonings as desired.

d. Reheat the keto crock pot chicken soup and serve it.

27. Cinnamon Caramel Almond Cake

Serves: 8

Cooking Time: 8 Minutes

Ingredients

- 2 oz. of butter (soft)
- 5 oz. of sugar
- 1 cup of almond flour
- 1 teaspoon of baking powder
- ¼ teaspoon of baking soda
- ¼ teaspoon of salt
- 1 tablespoon of cinnamon powder
- 1 teaspoon of vanilla
- 1 egg
- 1 cup of Greek yogurt, caramel (full fat)

‖‖

How to Cook:

a. Grease a 9-inch layer cake tin with cooking spray or some oil and sprinkle it with a little almond flour. Heat the oven to a temperature of 375°F.

b. Sift your cinnamon powder, salt, baking soda, baking powder, almond flour, and sugar in a large bowl. Stir to combine these ingredients and set the mixture aside.

c. In a blender, place the egg, butter, sugar, banana, and vanilla. Blend these ingredients for a period of 1 minute at super speed; by now, the consistency should be smooth.

d. Pour the blended mixture into the almond flour mixture and mix these together thoroughly.

e. Pour and scrape the batter into the greased tin. Place the tin in the oven and bake it for a period of 25 mins. Once this time has passed, remove the tin from the oven, leave the cinnamon caramel almond cake to cool and then serve it.

28. Butternut Squash Bisque

Makes: 12 Servings

Cooking Time: 1 Hour 20 Minutes

Ingredient List:

- Coconut oil (1 tablespoon)
- Sweet onions (2 medium, chopped)
- Leek (1, whites only, sliced
- Garlic (1 tablespoon, chopped)
- Butternut squash (3 lbs., peeled & cubed)
- Vegetable/chicken stock (1 qt.)
- Cinnamon (2 teaspoons, divided)
- Salt (1 teaspoon)
- Pepper (½ teaspoons)
- Raw pecans (¼ cup, chopped)

||||||||||||||||||||||||||||||||||||||||||||||||||||||||||||||||||||||||||||||

How to Cook:

a. In a stock pot, over medium flame, heat up the oil. Sauté the onion, leek, and garlic until the vegetables are soft (for roughly a period of 5-10 mins).

b. Add the apple and squash and cook the vegetables for a further period of 5 minutes. Pour in the stock, add a teaspoon of cinnamon and let it boil.

c. Cover the pot with a lid, and simmer the mixture on a reduced heat setting for a period of 45 minutes.

d. Blend the soup in a blender until it is smooth. Season as desired with salt and pepper.

e. Stir the pecans in with the other teaspoon of cinnamon. Sauté them lightly until they are fragrant (for a period of 4-5 mins).

f. Serve the butternut squash soup garnished with toasted, spiced pecans on top.

29. Classic Tricolor Salad

Serves: 2

Cooking Time: 8 Minutes

Ingredient List:

- Medium tomatoes (4 medium)
- Avocado (1 large)
- Olives (8)
- Mozzarella cheese (4.4 oz., "regular")
- Pesto (2 tablespoons Preferably homemade)
- Extra virgin olive oil (2 tablespoons)
- Salt, pepper, and fresh basil (for garnishing and seasoning, optional)

||||||||||||||||||||||||||||||||||||||||||||||||||||||||||||||||||||||||||||||

How to Cook:

a. Wash the tomatoes and slice them.

b. Cut the avocado into halves, deseed, peel and slice them.

c. Cut the olives in halves and remove the seeds. Place all of the vegetables in a serving bowl.

d. Add the mozzarella pieces, olive oil, and pesto

e. Season the salad with salt, fresh basil, and black pepper according to personal preference. These are optional. Now - enjoy!

30. Creamy Low-Carb Red Gazpacho

Makes: 6 Servings

Cooking Time: 40 Minutes

Ingredient List:

- Green peppers (1 large)
- Red peppers (1 large)
- Red onion (1 small)
- Avocados (2 medium)
- Medium tomatoes (5)
- Garlic (2 cloves)
- Fresh lemon juice (2 tablespoons)
- Apple cider vinegar (2 tablespoons)
- Basil (4 tablespoons Freshly chopped)
- Parsley (4 tablespoons Freshly chopped)
- Cucumber (1 large)
- Spring onions (2 medium)
- Salt to taste
- Freshly ground black pepper
- Extra virgin olive oil (1 cup)
- Feta cheese (200g)

||||||||||||||||||||||||||||||||||||||||||||||||||||||||||||||||||||||

How to Cook:

a. Heat the oven to a temperature of 400°F (280°C).

b. Splice the peppers in halves and remove the entire core with seeds.

c. On a baking sheet that has been lined with parchment paper, place the pepper halves with their cut side down and put them in the preheated oven.

d. The peppers should take a period of 20 minutes to be fully roas It is done when the skin blisters and becomes black.

e. In the meanwhile, peel the red onion, chop it and place it in a blender. Cut the tomatoes into 4 sections. Cut the avocados into halves, remove the seed, peel, and add them to the blender.

f. When the peppers have completed cooking, remove them from the oven and leave them to cool. When the peppers have cooled, peel off the skin and throw it away. Add the peppers to the blender.

g. Add the fresh herbs, lemon juice, peeled garlic, pepper, vinegar, salt, and olive oil to the blender as well (save some for garnishing).

h. Process all of the ingredients in a blender until they are smooth. Keep some olive oil for garnish. Slice the spring onions and dice the cucumber.

i. Add the spring onions and cucumber to the puree and mix until they are well combined. Add more salt and pepper if necessary.

j. Pour the soup into serving bowls, and top it with fresh herbs, feta cheese, and a dribble of olive oil. Serve the soup i It can be refrigerated for up to 5 days. Enjoy!

Author's Afterthoughts

Merci! That's French for "thank you"! And that's all I can say for how grateful I am for your support. Maybe you've been with me since my first publication, or maybe you recently stumbled upon my work — but I can only say thank you.

Now is the moment of truth, though. What did you think of my recipes? Be sure to let me know here or via Amazon or wherever you purchased my book from, because I read all of my reviews. Knowing what you thought of my cookbook is extremely important for improving my future books and recipes. Were the recipes too hard? Were the ingredients easy to find? Tell me everything!

After all, as a chef and cookbook writer, I want to be making recipes you actually like and can make with local ingredients. If you need to ship a fancy ingredient from the other side of the world and it's 2 weeks of shipping for it, well — by the time it arrives on your doorstep, you probably already forgot what it was for.

Let me know the good and the bad, I'm all ears.

Thanks!

Remi Morris

About the Author

Remi likes to joke that his name is just like that of Ratatouille's main character for a reason and no one challenges the claim. You see, Remi has always been a culinary mastermind for those surrounding him. When he was five, he prepared fig and brie sandwiches as his school lunch. In middle school, he baked raspberry and dulce de leche cupcakes and sold them around the neighborhood. Throughout high school, he cooked private dinners, even cooking for the town mayor twice!

Thus, when Remi left for France in 2010 on a backpacking trip, no one was surprised to hear from him 2 weeks later saying he'd been offered a job at a famous restaurant there. He met the restaurant owner at the supermarket, grabbing his attention with the selection of products in his cart and then watching as Remi explained to the cashier what he hoped to make for dinner. While the cashier wasn't interested in Remi's dinner plans, the restaurant owner was sure to follow up with Remi outside the store. Remi was told to stop by the restaurant if he wanted to learn more about the cuisine. The next day, Remi set foot in the restaurant at 9:00 am and walked out at 10:00 pm with a job offer in hand.

Remi stayed in Paris for nine years, where he perfected his craft and began working on his first cookbook, a compilation of impressive fine dining recipes. Published in 2013 and receiving huge praise, Remi decided to move back to Orange County in California and continue publishing cookbooks based on his experience in France. Now, Remi lives with his partner, Samantha, and their 2 turtles, Eclair and Stitch.

Made in United States
Orlando, FL
15 April 2024

4583744OR00041